Magnolia

A Life Rooted in Faith

DR. WILLIAM EPPS JR.

Scripture References

Scripture quotations marked NIV are taken from the Holy Bible, New International Version®, NIV®. Copyright © 1973, 1978, 1984, 2011 by Biblica, Inc.™ Used by permission. All rights reserved worldwide.

All additional Scripture quotations are from the public domain King James Version (KJV), where indicated. Printed in the United States of America.

CONTENTS

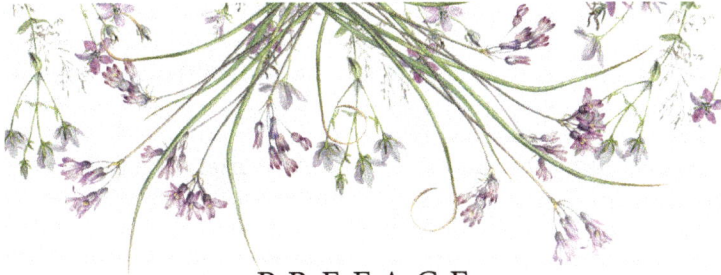

PREFACE

This book was not written solely to preserve memories but to bear witness to a life rooted in God. It is a testimony shaped by love, faith, and lived experience. At its heart is a woman whose life quietly pointed others toward peace, healing, and a relationship with the Father.

These pages are based on private conversations, personal reflections, and audio recordings that captured her story—a life lived in worship, grounded in humility and grace. They reflect moments, lessons, and truths passed down through generations. They are written not to elevate a person, but to honor the God who shaped her character, guided her steps, and carried her faithfully through every season of life. What you will read is not an account of perfection, but of devotion. Not a story of ease, but of trust.

Throughout this book, I refer to her as Magnolia O. Epps. In my life, I have only ever called her Grandma — and I always will. But in these pages, I've chosen to use her name to honor her as a full and complex woman of God, beyond her role within our family. This decision is meant to give voice to her testimony as a woman, a disciple, and a living witness to the goodness of God.

At her service, two songs captured the essence of her faith. One reflected a longing for the nearness of Christ, a heart posture that continually invited Jesus to draw close, to meet us in waiting, weariness, and hope. That longing marked her life. She lived with an awareness of God's presence and an expectation that He would meet her in every season.

The other song testified to grace and mercy — the unearned kindness of God that sustains, forgives, restores, and carries us when strength fails. She understood that it was not her own goodness that held her, but the grace of God. Mercy covered her past, steadied her present, and secured her future.

Together, these themes tell her story. She lived with a heart turned toward Jesus and a life anchored in grace. She trusted Christ's nearness and rested in God's mercy. In doing so, she modeled a faith that was not rooted in fear or obligation, but in love, trust, and relationship.

This book is meant to be read slowly. It is part remembrance, part reflection, and part invitation — an invitation to consider faith as a relationship rather than a ritual, to see healing as a journey rather than an event, and to recognize the quiet ways God moves through ordinary lives.

If these words stir remembrance, encourage faith, or open space for reflection, then they have served their purpose. May this testimony point you not only to a remarkable life, but to the God whose grace and mercy make all things whole.

WITH GRATITUDE

Before this story continues, it is important to honor two lives whose love made her final years a sacred season.

For the last nine years of her life, my grandmother was cared for in the home of my father and mother, who served as her full-time caregivers. They did so not out of obligation, but out of love, reverence, and deep respect for the woman who had given so much to our family. Their care was marked by patience, sacrifice, and unwavering commitment. They provided her with dignity, comfort, protection, and peace, ensuring that her final season was one of presence rather than loneliness.

There was also a uniquely beautiful bond between mother and son, a relationship that spanned sixty-five years. It was a bond shaped by trust, loyalty, and love, and in her final years, it came full circle as he honored her through faithful care. Alongside him stood the steady, nurturing love of a wife and daughter-in-law, whose compassion and devotion made their home a place of safety and rest.

Their caregiving was an extension of her legacy.

Their love was a continuation of her testimony.

For that, and for the countless unseen sacrifices made along the way, this book is written with deep gratitude.

CHAPTER 1

Faith Before the Fruit

Before she became Mama, Grandma, or Miss Maggie of West Baltimore, she was Magnolia Olive Brogdon of Manning, South Carolina — a girl raised by the land, shaped by the Spirit, and guided by a faith that took root long before she ever fully understood its depth. Born on July 22, 1933, to Samuel and Viola Brogdon, Magnolia entered a world marked by hardship and segregation, yet her childhood was rich with dignity, purpose, and spiritual heritage.

Her parents had only a simple formal education, but the education of the Spirit was in their bones. They carried Scripture not in books alone, but in their hearts. Verses were woven into their conversations, their decisions, their discipline, and their parenting. They lived a Spirit-led, Jesus-centered life, creating an atmosphere of reverence and peace in their home. Magnolia often explained that her parents didn't just know the Bible—they embodied it. Their faith shaped the rhythm of their days and the posture of their hearts.

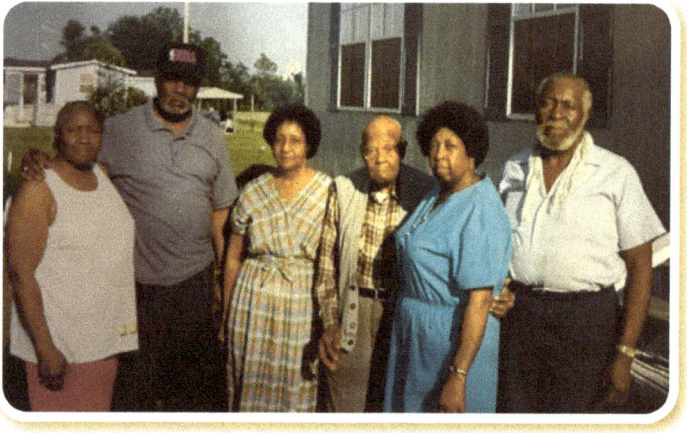

Magnolia with her father and siblings.

The Brogdon family managed a working farm. Life began before sunrise, tending to animals, feeding livestock, and nurturing crops in the South Carolina soil. Magnolia learned early that the land responds to what you put into it — prayer, diligence, patience, and love. But in her family, farming was also an act of worship. Her parents practiced the biblical principle of first fruits: before anything was eaten, stored, or sold, they gave the very first of every crop back to God.

Whether it was the first tomato, the first handful of greens, or the first produce of the season, they would set it aside as a thank-you offering. This simple, sacred practice taught Magnolia a lifelong truth:

Everything you plant with God grows beyond its natural strength.

Those years laid the spiritual foundation of her life — a faith disciplined, obedient, and deeply relational.

But the most defining moment of her youth did not happen in the fields. It happened inside the sanctuary of Biggers AME Church, the church her family helped to build. At fourteen, Magnolia gave her life to Christ in an experience so profound that it marked her Spirit forever.

She would recount it often, her voice softening with the memory. The Holy Spirit fell on her in such power that it moved her across the sanctuary. She began on one side of the church and, hours later, found herself in the far corner on the floor, overwhelmed, weeping, and wrapped in the presence of God. Time slipped away. All she knew was that God had touched her — and nothing would ever be the same.

From that moment, Magnolia didn't simply believe in God; she walked with Him. She trusted Him. She listened for His voice. Her encounter at fourteen became her anchor through every season that followed — marriage, motherhood, hardship, moving, and loss.

As she grew older, her faith shaped all she became. When King David Epps began courting her, he pursued a young woman rooted in conviction, humility, and strength. Their marriage became the foundation of a large, loving family. Together, they raised eight children, and Magnolia embraced motherhood as holy work. Her home was built on prayer, Scripture, discipline, and love — the same foundation her parents had given her.

In 1952, Magnolia and her young family moved to Baltimore, Maryland. The transition from rural farmland to city living was dramatic, yet she carried her heritage with her — the spiritual strength of Manning, the lessons of the land, and the faith sealed in her heart as a teenager.

She worked first as a housekeeper, then as a senior nursing aide at the University of Maryland Hospital, and ultimately as a Licensed Practical Nurse in the ICU at Maryland General Hospital. She cared for patients with compassion, gentleness, and unwavering commitment. For Magnolia, nursing was not just a profession; it was a ministry.

Her love for ministry extended far beyond her workplace. She served faithfully in church — at Ebenezer AME Church, then Fulton Avenue Baptist Church, where she became a Sunday School teacher and missionary. Her influence reached people she never met through the prayers she prayed, the lessons she taught, and the seeds of faith she planted everywhere she went.

Her home became a sanctuary for family, neighbors, children, and strangers alike. If you crossed her threshold, you were fed, welcomed, listened to, and loved. Children found safety in her presence. Her fried chicken, coconut pies, and molasses cakes became legendary. Her stoop became a place of early morning devotion, where she sat with a cup of coffee and multiple Bibles in arm's reach.

And even in the heart of West Baltimore — surrounded by pavement, rowhomes, and city noise — Magnolia made life grow. She built a garden on the sidewalk, planting seeds where most people only saw concrete. With prayer, patience, and determination, she coaxed greens, vegetables, and tomatoes out of a patch of earth she constructed with her own hands. People often shook their heads in amazement, but Magnolia knew the secret: she tended that garden like she tended people — with love, faith, and consistency.

Her garden became a symbol of her life:

Life blooming where it should not be able to grow,

faith flourishing on hard ground,

And nourishment springing out of places overlooked by others.

She experienced more loss than most hearts could bear, yet she held onto her faith with quiet strength. Her resilience came not from willpower but from the God who met her in a small country church when she was fourteen. Her love for her children, grandchildren, great-grandchildren, and the many she unofficially adopted was unwavering. She walked the streets of West Baltimore with children following behind her, leading them to Sunday School and teaching them how to pray, honor God, and love themselves.

Her story does not begin with her passing, nor does it end there. Magnolia's life is defined by the faith she lived, the love she gave, and the legacy she planted in every heart she touched. From the farmland of Manning to the streets of Baltimore, her life bore fruit — spiritual, emotional, communal — that continues to multiply.

This book begins not with her death, but with her foundation:

The girl raised on a Southern farm,

The teenager touched by the Holy Spirit,

The mother guided by prayer,

The nurse who cared with compassion,

The missionary who served with humility,

And the matriarch whose life continues to bear fruit long after her hands stopped tending the soil.

This is Magnolia.

And this is the legacy from which every chapter grows.

CHAPTER 2

Scripture in Her Bones

Some people read the Bible.

Some people study the Bible.

But every so often, God raises someone who becomes the Bible in motion. Someone whose life reflects Scripture so consistently that the Word is no longer something they quote—it is something they carry, live, breathe, and embody. This was Magnolia.

From her earliest days in Manning, Scripture was the backdrop of her life. Her parents, Samuel and Viola, did not have the benefit of extensive formal education, but spiritually they were scholars, pillars, and teachers. They preached the Gospel through the way they lived. They had Scripture hidden so deeply in their hearts that it became the very tone of their household.

Their conversations wove in passages of the Bible. Their discipline mirrored biblical principles. Their gratitude to God shaped their routine. They rose early, worked hard, and honored God in the small things. And they practiced the biblical principle of first fruits with unwavering faithfulness. Before a single vegetable or crop was eaten, sold, or stored, they gave the very first portion back to God. "Honor the Lord with your wealth, with the firstfruits of all your crops" (Proverbs 3:9 NIV). To them, this was not a ritual. It was a declaration of dependence. It was a proclamation that everything they had came from the hand of God.

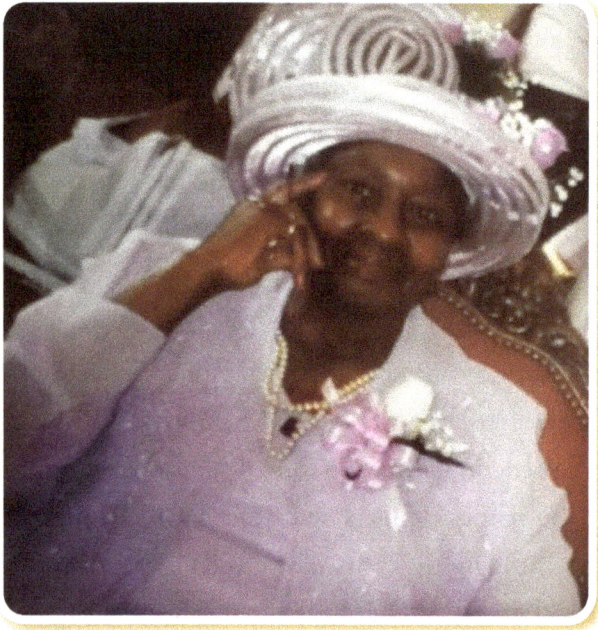

Magnolia on Mother's Day.

Magnolia saw this as a child, and it shaped her entire understanding of Scripture. She watched her parents tithe not only money but also harvest. She watched them pray over the land. She watched them trust God through droughts and storms. She watched them open their home to others because they believed generosity was the fruit of righteousness.

Those early lessons taught Magnolia that obedience is not merely doing what God says—it is trusting the heart behind His instructions. It is recognizing that Scripture is not a rulebook but a way of living.

As she grew, Scripture became her lifelong companion. She did not travel without a Bible. Ever. Whether she was heading to work, going to church, visiting family, or riding through the city, a Bible was always near. It was in her purse. On her nightstand. Under her arm. On the passenger seat. Sitting open on the dining room table. Wherever Magnolia was, the Word was within reach.

One day she said, "As long as I have the Word, I have everything I need."

This was not a slogan for her. It was the truth she built her life upon.

She believed deeply in the power of Scripture—not as literature, but as living revelation. And she shared that belief with everyone she encountered. You could not talk to Magnolia and walk away without a seed planted. She brought Scripture into conversations the way a musician brings rhythm into a song—naturally, instinctively, effortlessly. It flowed from her because it lived in her.

If you were discouraged, she had a verse.

If you were confused, she had a lesson.

If you were rebellious, she had correction.

If you needed clarity, she had revelation.

If you needed encouragement, she had prayer.

Her ministry was constant, quiet, and woven into everyday life. She was not a preacher with a pulpit. She was a messenger with a daily assignment: steward the Word and deliver it to those who needed it.

Psalm 23 was one of her anchors. She quoted it frequently:

"The Lord is my shepherd; I shall not want" (Psalm 23:1 NIV).

This verse wasn't comfort to her; it was identity. God's leadership was her security. God's provision was her assurance. God's presence was her peace.

Her reverence for the Ten Commandments shaped her character. She lived with moral clarity, integrity, and humility. She believed boundaries were blessings. She believed obedience protected the soul. She believed holiness mattered.

As Magnolia aged, Scripture only grew stronger within her. When she was diagnosed with dementia, many expected her spiritual memory to fade with her physical one. But she had already settled this in her heart. She told me, "God already showed me this season. My physical memory may go, but spiritually the Word will never leave me." She firmly believed that the enemy could not steal what God Himself had planted.

And she proved it.

Even as her mind shifted, her Spirit remained anchored. She sometimes forgot names, but never forgot God. She forgot the day of the week, but never forgot to pray. She forgot appointments, but never forgot Scripture.

Psalm 139 lived in her. She could recite it word for word in her final season.

"O Lord, you have searched me, and you know me" (Psalm 139:1 NIV).

"If I make my bed in the depths, you are there" (Psalm 139:8 NIV).

"I praise you because I am fearfully and wonderfully made" (Psalm 139:14 NIV).

How could she keep Scripture when her memory could not keep other things?

Spiritual memory is not stored in the mind.

It is stored in the Spirit.

It cannot be erased.

It cannot be altered.

It cannot be stolen.

Even in her weakness, Magnolia remained a watchman. Like the watchmen described in Scripture—those positioned on the walls to warn, to pray, to protect—she kept spiritual vigilance. She discerned shifts in the atmosphere. She prayed through the night. She covered her family with intercession. She saw what others missed. She felt spiritual storms before they arrived. Her calling was anchored in Scripture and fueled by prayer.

Her life teaches us a profound lesson:

We are called to carry the Word as she did.

We are called to steward Scripture deeply—so deeply that it becomes part of who we are. We are called to bring the Word into our conversations, our decisions, our relationships, our work, and our homes. We are called to plant seeds in others—not with pressure, not with force, but with love. We may not always be the ones to water those seeds, but God asks us to plant what we know.

A verse.

A prayer.

A truth.

A reminder.

A warning.

A word of hope.

Magnolia understood that Scripture is a gift meant to be shared. And she shared it generously. Her life invites us not only to admire her faith but also to imitate it.

We are called to carry the Word as she did.

To steward Scripture until it becomes part of who we are.

To plant seeds, trusting God to water them.

Magnolia's life invites us not just to remember her faith, but to walk in it.

Magnolia did not just know the Bible.

She carried it.

She lived it.

She breathed it.

She became it.

And she leaves us with this truth:

If you place the Word in your bones, it will carry you when everything else fails.

CHAPTER 3

The Code She Lived By

Magnolia did not simply believe in God. She lived in a way that reflected Him. Her faith was quiet but unwavering, steady, and deeply rooted. It did not demand recognition or applause. It was expressed through the code she lived by every day—a code shaped by honesty, purity, respect, and deep reverence for her Father in heaven.

She was a lady in every sense of the Word. Classy. Graceful. Composed. She carried herself with a dignity that needed no introduction. She did not raise her voice. She did not cuss. She did not speak to tear down or injure with her words. She believed that words create atmosphere and shift spiritual doors, so she guarded her tongue with intention. To her, controlling one's tongue was not repression. It was worship.

Her love showed up quietly, in the way she treated people with tenderness and dignity. She made people feel seen without drawing attention to herself. The love she carried was never loud. It was steady, consistent, and sincere. Her love invited people to breathe.

Her joy wasn't loud either. It lived in the soft warmth of her smile and the way her presence made a room feel lighter. It was a joy anchored in God, a joy that held firm even when life did not. Being around her felt like stepping into calm sunlight.

One of our favorite pictures of Magnolia.
She was known for her hats.

Peace went wherever she did. It clung to her like a fragrance. She carried a stillness that settled tension before she spoke a word. People relaxed around her without understanding why. The peace she carried was not a matter of personality. It was the evidence of a life rooted in prayer.

Patience shaped how she navigated people and seasons. Magnolia did not rush God, rush conversation, or rush relationships. She moved at the pace of grace. When others grew frustrated, she remained steady. Her patience was one of her greatest gifts because it allowed people to mature, heal, and unfold without pressure.

Alongside her patience lived another depth of character: long-suffering. She understood that long-suffering is the attitude a believer holds during waiting. It is the quiet decision to remain steady when life stretches you. It is the choice to trust God when answers are delayed, to stand firm without complaint, and to carry peace when frustration would have been justified. Magnolia lived this deeply. She stayed settled in seasons that would have broken others. She never rushed God. She waited well. She understood that the teacher does not always speak or provide the answers during the test, but watches.

Kindness shaped everything she did. She cooked meals for the hungry. She opened her doors to children. She offered help before anyone asked. Her kindness did not come from politeness but from compassion. Compassion was her natural posture.

Goodness governed her decisions long before anyone could see them. She lived with integrity that did not shift based on who was watching. Whether caring for a neighbor, handling conflict, or making personal decisions, her choices consistently reflected her faith. Righteousness wasn't something she talked about. It was something she practiced.

Her faithfulness carried her through every season of her life. She was faithful in prayer, steadfast in Scripture, faithful to church, loyal to family, and faithful in service. If she said she would do something, she did it. If she said she would pray for you, she meant it. Her faithfulness was quiet but powerful. It shaped the atmosphere of her home.

Gentleness marked her tone. Even when she corrected, she did so with softness. There was never sharpness in her voice, never a harsh edge, even when she needed to set something straight. She had a way of guiding you back into place without embarrassing you, belittling you, or raising her voice. Everyone in the family knew this about her. You could disappoint her, even frustrate her, but she would never meet you with anger. Instead, she spoke in that calm, steady way that made you feel both corrected and loved at the same time. It was not a weakness. It was not being soft. It was spiritual maturity. It was a woman who had mastered her Spirit. Her gentleness was her strength. It kept the conflict from growing. It softened hearts instead of hardening them. And because she never raised her voice, her whisper carried authority.

Self-control shaped her entire life. Magnolia believed that holiness was revealed in the moments no one applauded. She held her peace even when frustrated. She disciplined her reactions because she refused to dishonor God with careless words or impulsive behavior. She understood that controlling oneself is not about suppressing emotion but about honoring God above emotion. Often, all she needed to correct someone was a look — not harsh, but knowing — a look that said, "You know better." It was enough. Her restraint came from reverence, from understanding that the Holy Spirit is sensitive and that His presence rests on those who guard their Spirit with intention.

All of these qualities flowed from the same place: her relationship with God. She lived by Psalm 19:14, "May these words of my mouth and this meditation of my heart be pleasing in your sight, Lord, my Rock and my Redeemer" (NIV). She guarded her heart because she knew the mouth follows the heart.

Respect was foundational to her code. Respect for others. Respect for herself. Most of all, respect for God. She carried herself with dignity because she knew to whom she belonged. Her identity was shaped not by culture or trends but by righteousness. She did not have to work to shine. She shone because she walked with the Light.

Magnolia refused to fight battles that belonged to God. If someone mistreated her, she never sought retaliation. She believed her Father would handle those who mishandled her. She lived the truth of Romans 12:17 and 19 without needing to quote it. She believed silence, prayer, and integrity were stronger than retaliation. Her restraint came from trust, not fear.

Her purity was not outdated or rigid. It was essential. Purity of mind. Purity of heart. Purity of motives. Purity of conversation. She often reminded others that the Holy Spirit is sensitive and that His presence does not rest on a careless soul. She believed the anointing thrives in clean vessels.

Living by this code freed her. It freed her from bitterness, from retaliation, from unnecessary battles. It freed her to forgive quickly, to love deeply, and to trust God completely. It freed her to walk through life without carrying offense like a burden.

Her life invites us to embrace the same code.

To honor God with our words and our silence.

To recognize that every action is worship.

To walk in purity when the world celebrates compromise.

To respond with gentleness instead of aggression.

To trust God with our battles instead of fighting them ourselves.

Magnolia lived by a code written not on paper but on her heart. A code shaped by Scripture, refined by prayer, and upheld by the Spirit.

And she leaves us with this truth:

When you walk with honor, God fights for you.

When you speak with purity, heaven speaks through you.

When you live with reverence, your life becomes worship.

Her code was simple.

Her code was holy.

Her code was powerful.

And her code continues to teach us how to live.

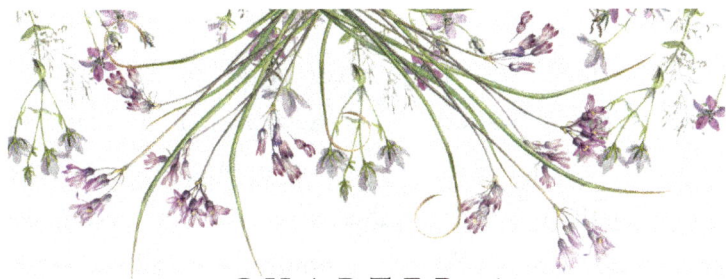

CHAPTER 4

The Watchman Anointing

Some believers pray, and then there are those who are assigned to pray. Magnolia was one of the latter. She carried the mantle of an intercessor long before anyone taught her the Word. It was the gift God planted in her Spirit, the assignment she fulfilled quietly, faithfully, and without applause. She walked the earth as a watchman — one who saw, one who sensed, one who stood guard in the Spirit when others slept.

Intercessors are Heaven's first responders. They are spiritually alert, discerning, sensitive to God's voice, and obedient to His prompting. Magnolia lived this calling with reverence. She could feel when someone in the family was in danger. She could sense when a storm was coming — not the kind made of wind, but the kind that shakes households. She discerned shifts in the spiritual realm the way others discern changes in the weather. And she responded the way a watchman is called to respond: with prayer.

She understood that intercession is not casual prayer. Intercession is warfare. It is advocacy. It is standing between heaven and earth for someone who may not have the strength to stand for themselves. At her service, we explained it through the courtroom image we all recognize. In courtrooms, the defense attorney stands by the accused, speaking on their behalf, presenting their case, and shielding them from condemnation.

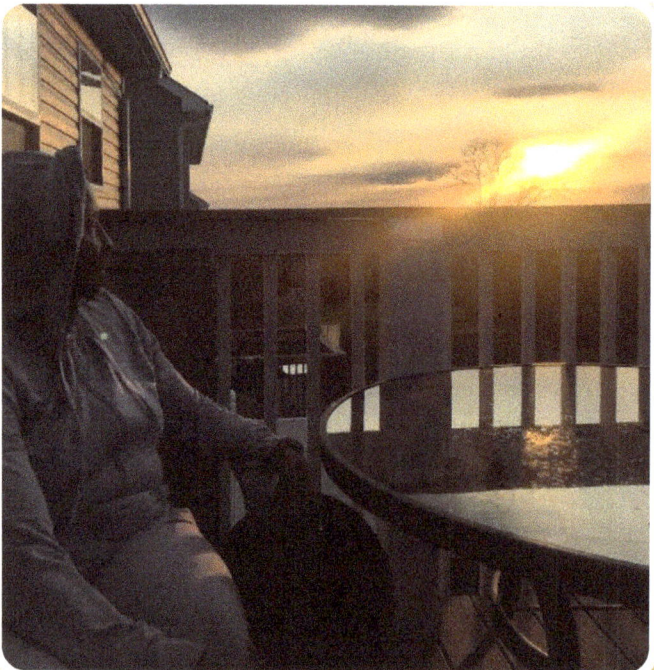

Magnolia sitting on my porch looking at a sunset.

When Jesus ascended to the right hand of the Father, Scripture says He became exactly that for us. Our eternal Advocate. Our Defender. Our Intercessor. "Christ Jesus… is at the right hand of God and is also interceding for us" (Romans 8:34 NIV). Intercessors on earth reflect this same assignment. God gives some of His children the responsibility of standing in the gap for others. Their lives look different. Their nights look different. Their prayers sound different. They carry burdens not their own, pray for people they've never met, and fight battles in the Spirit that others will never know about.

Magnolia lived this calling. She paced the floors at night when the Spirit stirred her. She woke up at unusual hours with someone's face or name in her Spirit. Sometimes she didn't know the person. Sometimes she didn't know the situation. She only knew God was calling her to intercede, and she answered. She prayed until peace came. She prayed until the heaviness lifted. She prayed until the burden broke. She prayed until God told her to stop. Whether the person lived next door or on the other side of the world, she warred for them as if they were her own blood.

Intercessors often pray without details. God gives them impressions, visions, or a sudden heaviness that does not belong to them. Magnolia responded without hesitation. She believed that obedience in prayer activates angelic protection. She understood Psalm 91, that "He will command His angels concerning you" (Psalm 91:11 NIV). She knew her prayers released ministry angels into warfare on behalf of those who lacked the strength or awareness to fight.

This calling shaped how she carried herself—alert, discerning, spiritually aware. She never walked blindly into a day. She sensed things. She watched the spiritual landscape the way the ancient watchmen stood on walls, scanning for danger, guarding the people, and sounding the alarm. Ezekiel 33 speaks of the watchman's responsibility, and Magnolia lived this with quiet devotion. She stood on the wall for our family. She stood guard over generations with prayer.

Her discernment did not come from anxiety. It came from intimacy with God. She listened in the Spirit. She watched in the Spirit. She prayed in the Spirit. And because of this, she walked with a confidence rooted not in herself, but in the God who saw all.

Intercessors also live clothed in the Armor of God, not visibly but spiritually. Magnolia wore this armor daily. She fastened the belt of truth around her waist by living honestly and speaking Scripture. She walked in the breastplate of righteousness through her lifestyle of purity. Her feet were fitted with the Gospel of peace — everywhere she went, she carried serenity with her. She lifted the shield of faith whenever fear tried to rise, refusing to let doubt extinguish what God had promised. Her helmet of salvation never slipped; she did not waver in her identity. And the sword of the Spirit, the Word of God, lived on her tongue and in her heart. Even as dementia touched her memory, Scripture remained untouched. She quoted scripture, verse after verse with accuracy, even when faces escaped her memory. The Word was written so deeply in her Spirit that no illness could erase it.

Even toward the end of her life, when her memory began to fade, her Spirit remained steadfast. My parents would often say that even when she could no longer remember names or faces, they would still hear her softly whispering the names of her children, grandchildren, and great-grandchildren in prayer. She prayed for each generation as if they stood right before her. Even as her mind released details, her Spirit held its assignment. She continued to stand on the wall, praying, warring, and filling the gap for our family and for people whose faces she had never known. Her body remained in a posture of prayer until the very end.

This is the life of an intercessor — someone who stands so close to God that spiritual truth becomes muscle memory.

She also understood the profound security of God's love. Intercessors carry this assurance because they need it to endure spiritual battles on behalf of others. Magnolia lived the truth of Romans 8:38–39:

> "For I am convinced that neither death
> nor life, neither angels nor demons,

neither the present nor the future, nor any powers… will be able to separate us from the love of God that is in Christ Jesus our Lord" (NIV).

This verse wasn't a theory to her. It was truth. It was an anchor. It was the foundation beneath her intercession. She prayed, trusting that nothing could sever the people she covered from the love of God she was calling down over them. She prayed, knowing heaven was listening. She prayed, knowing God fought for those she fought for.

Her watchman's anointing was not loud. It was not dramatic. It was not advertised. It was steady, holy, and relentless. She prayed because she believed prayer was a partnership with heaven.

Magnolia was a spiritual wall around our family.

A shield.

A guard.

A covering.

Her prayers built spiritual fortresses over generations.

And now her life calls us to step into the same posture — to stand in the gap, to watch, to discern, to intercede, to listen, to obey, and to cover others with the same love Christ covers us with at the right hand of the Father.

The mantle she carried does not disappear.

It is passed.

The Truth is:

Her prayers are still standing.

Her covering is still working.

Her legacy is still warring.

Furthermore nothing, not death, not memory loss, not time, can separate us from the love of God she prayed over us, or from the God who still hears us.

CHAPTER 5

What a Friend We Have in Jesus

Some hymns are sung. Others are lived.

For Magnolia, "What a Friend We Have in Jesus" was not just a melody—it was the story of her life. It was the soundtrack of her walk with God, the quiet declaration of how she endured storms, carried burdens, and found rest in the presence of a Savior who never left her side.

She believed in Jesus not only as Lord, but as Friend. A true and faithful Friend. A Friend who carries what we cannot lift, holds what we cannot hold, and comforts in ways no human heart is capable of offering. Magnolia lived this truth the way some people breathe — instinctively, daily, without needing to think about it. Friendship with Jesus was her lifeline, her anchor, and her place of refuge.

She believed wholeheartedly in a Savior who willingly bears our sorrows and stands with us in grief. When life broke her heart, she carried that heartbreak straight to Him. She did not run from God; she ran toward Him. She refused to let bitterness take root. She refused to let anger replace faith. She trusted the One who promised to carry every burden she released to Him.

Magnolia understood something many believers miss:

Friendship with Jesus does not remove suffering — it transforms it.

Magnolia standing on her stoop next to
her snowball stand on Easter Day.

It pulls you through what should have destroyed you.

It steadies you when life becomes unrecognizable.

It reminds you that you are never carrying anything alone.

And Magnolia lived that truth with quiet strength.

She believed wholeheartedly in the privilege of bringing everything to God. When the family faced trouble, she prayed. When someone was sick, she prayed. When danger loomed, she prayed. When the world felt heavy, she prayed. Even when memory faded, she continued praying — faithfully, instinctively, automatically.

Prayer was not something she did. Prayer was who she was. It was the posture of her life. She understood prayer as an ongoing conversation with her friend.

And so, when we ask how she remained faithful through all she endured, the answer is simple:

She knew God not only as Father, Creator, Healer, and Provider — she knew Him as Friend.

This chapter invites us to rediscover that truth for ourselves.

We celebrate God's power, but we often forget His proximity. He is not distant. He desires connection, communion, and relationship. He desires friendship.

A friend is one who shows affection, loyalty, kindness, and support, someone who chooses you and walks beside you. But the Bible takes friendship deeper.

The Greek Word phílos means "beloved" or "dear one," and from it comes philia, the love of friendship — a love marked by loyalty and shared life. It is the love that stays present, shares burdens, and walks alongside someone through every season.

This is the Word Jesus uses in John 15 (NIV) when He says, "I have called you friends."

A servant obeys without relationship.

A friend responds from relationship.

Jesus invites us into closeness — into shared heart and shared purpose.

This is why many believers throughout Scripture viewed God personally. Abraham was called God's friend — not because he was perfect, but because he believed God, trusted God, and walked with God. His obedience flowed from relationship. That is biblical friendship — covenantal, intentional, faithful.

And that same friendship is offered to us today.

Many of us, however, experience God only as Father but never embrace Him as Friend.

We honor His authority but do not lean into His companionship.

We respect His sovereignty but never allow ourselves to enjoy His closeness.

There is a difference:

A Father covers you;

a Friend walks with you.

A Father provides;

a Friend participates.

A Father gives instruction;

a Friend gives comfort.

A Father leads;

a Friend listens.

Many believers stay stuck in a servant-Master dynamic, never stepping into the friendship Jesus offered. Friends share hearts. Friends share burdens. Friends respond with affection instead of obligation. Friends rest in being loved instead of worrying about being enough.

Even as parents, we understand this tension — we struggle to be both parent and friend to our children. We wrestle with discipline and closeness, guidance and connection. But God balances these perfectly.

He is both Father and Friend — powerful and personal, holy and near, sovereign and intimate.

Magnolia understood that balance.

She lived in the security of a Father who covered her,

And she walked in the intimacy of a Friend who stayed with her.

That is why her faith remained firm.

That is why her strength seemed supernatural.

That is why her peace remained unshakable.

She did not worship a distant God; she walked with a present One.

She did not merely pray to a King; she conversed with a Friend.

And that friendship carried her through every storm.

Magnolia knew trials intimately. She buried her children. She endured hardship that would have broken many. But her Friend sustained her. He walked with her. He held her. He whispered strength into places grief tried to hollow out. She believed — truly believed — that "God will carry you through anything if you let Him."

She lived that truth.

Even as dementia touched her mind, her spiritual memory remained anchored in friendship with God. She still prayed. She still whispered the names of her children, grandchildren, and great-grandchildren, sometimes when she could no longer recall their faces. Her body forgot many things — but it never forgot her Friend.

That is the mark of a life lived in divine companionship.

Some of us today have forfeited peace.

Some of us carry pain we do not have to carry.

Some of us bear burdens we were never meant to lift alone.

Why?

Because we have not taken them to our Friend in prayer.

Magnolia never forfeited her peace. She knew the One who would get her through every situation. She leaned on His presence, trusted His nearness, and rested in His companionship until the very end.

She left this world the way she lived in it —

In conversation with her Friend.

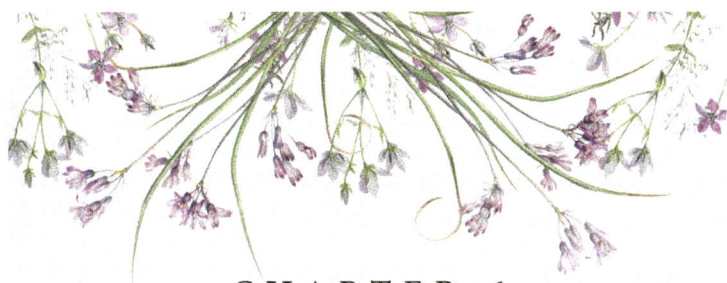

CHAPTER 6

A Home of Healing

Some people build houses. Magnolia built a refuge. Her home was not defined by its walls, its furniture, or its size. It was characterized by its Spirit and warmth. The moment you stepped into her space — whether it was her childhood home in Manning, her stoop on Baltimore Street, or her kitchen filled with pots and pans — there was a sense of calm that settled over you. A relief. A softening. A release. Her home felt like exhaling after holding your breath too long. It felt like being reminded that you were safe, seen, and loved.

Her hospitality was not learned; it was anointed. Magnolia carried a spiritual gift that turned ordinary moments into sacred ones. It was not about the things she had. It was about the presence she carried. People felt God's nearness in her house. They felt the gentleness of the Holy Spirit in her voice. They felt peace in her kitchen, comfort stitched into her quilts, and love simmering in every pot she prepared..

Her children brought friends home who would go on to call her "Mama" too—not because they needed another parent, but because something in her presence felt like home. She made room for people not just physically, but emotionally and spiritually. She embraced without hesitation. She welcomed without judgment. She listened without rushing. Her presence carried an unconditional acceptance that allowed people to lay down their armor and simply be.

Magnolia with all her children.

Her home became a hospital of love and support. This was not metaphorical — it was lived. People who were depressed, overwhelmed, heartbroken, or confused came to her house, and somehow, they left lighter. She healed many without medicine — through prayer, through wisdom, through empathy, through simple acts of kindness that carried spiritual power. Some came to her home with tears. Some came with silence. Some came with burdens they could not tell anyone else. Magnolia met every one of them exactly where they were.

She poured into people without asking for anything in return, offering a warm plate of food, a quiet prayer whispered over someone as they rested, and a seat at her table with no expectation of performing or pretending. Her home was a sanctuary for weary souls. People would stop by just to sit near her because peace lived inside her. She made the broken feel whole, the lost feel found, and the overwhelmed feel understood.

And just as she cared for the emotionally and spiritually wounded, she also cared for the physically weak. Magnolia walked with many people until their final breath. Not only family members but also neighbors, church members, and individuals who had no one else. She sat beside them when others could not. She held hands when fragile life needed gentleness. She prayed when voices had grown too weak to speak. She offered presence when fear would have otherwise filled the room. She took care of many people until they crossed from this life into eternity, making sure they did not leave this world alone. She was a midwife to the soul—helping people transition into God's peace.

This was not a burden to her. It was worship.

She understood Matthew 25:40 in a way most people read but never live: "Whatever you did for the least of these, you did for Me." To Magnolia, caring for people was not a chore. It was a calling. Feeding people was a ministry. Listening was a ministry. Sitting with the dying was a ministry. Her hands, her voice, her home — all of it belonged to God.

Her home carried the presence of the Holy Spirit because she carried Him within herself. There was no need for signs or religious theatrics. The evidence was in the peace people felt when they walked in. The evidence was in the love that settled on them like a warm blanket. The evidence was in her consistency — the same gentle tone, the same welcoming smile, the same posture of prayer day after day.

People came to her with anger and left with clarity.

They came with grief and left with strength.

They came with burdens and left with hope.

They came lost and left guided.

She fed not only stomachs but spirits. A meal at her table was never just food. It was fellowship. It was comfort. It was healing. It was spiritual nourishment disguised as Southern cooking.

Magnolia lived Isaiah 58 without ever quoting it — the call to share bread with the hungry, to shelter the wanderer, to lift burdens, to break yokes. Her home was a place where yokes broke quietly through kindness and consistency rather than force or judgment.

Her ministry was not in a pulpit. It was in her living room. It was on her front stoop. It was in her kitchen, where she stirred prayers into pots and love into every plate she served. It was in the countless conversations she held at her table, conversations that healed hearts more deeply than any sermon could.

She understood that ministry does not require a title. Love is the most significant credential. Compassion is the greatest authority. Service is the most excellent sermon.

Magnolia's home teaches us something important:

Healing does not always require miracles.

Sometimes healing is present.

Sometimes healing is consistent.

Sometimes healing is warmth.

Sometimes healing is a safe place to sit and breathe.

Her home was not perfect, but it was holy.

Not extravagant, but abundant.

Not large, but expansive in Spirit.

What made her home special was not what was inside it — but who was inside it.

God was there because she invited Him.

Love was there because she carried it.

Peace was there because she lived it.

And all who entered were changed by it.

Her legacy now challenges us to consider the ministries we overlook. Who are we feeding? Who are we comforting? Who feels safe in our presence? Who finds healing in our homes? Who senses God when they encounter us?

A home that heals does not require wealth.

It requires warmth.

It requires willingness.

It requires love.

Magnolia gave all three freely.

And because she did, her home became holy ground.

CHAPTER 7

The Legacy that Heals

At the core of Magnolia's life was one truth: she wanted people to know her Father. Not as an idea, not as a distant deity, not as a religious concept — but personally. Intimately. Relationally. She wanted people to know the God who walked with her through childhood in South Carolina, through motherhood in Baltimore, through grief, joy, hardship, and victory. She wanted them to know the God who healed her, guided her, strengthened her, and carried her—the God she trusted with every breath.

Her legacy was not just one of kindness, service, and hospitality. Her legacy was that of an evangelist — one who carried the Gospel in her footsteps, in her conversations, in her prayers, and in the atmosphere she nurtured wherever she went. Magnolia preached without needing a pulpit. Her life was her sermon. Her character was her Scripture. Her healing touch was her altar call.

She believed wholeheartedly in the healing power of God, physical, emotional, and spiritual. She lived the truth of Psalm 147:3 (NIV): "He heals the brokenhearted and binds up their wounds." She witnessed God restore what seemed broken beyond repair, comfort hearts that ached deeply, and lift burdens that had weighed on people for years. She knew healing was real because she had experienced it, and she wanted others to know they could experience it too.

Magnolia believed that peace came from God alone — not momentary calm, not temporary relief, but deep, sustaining peace that remained even when life shook. She lived Proverbs 3:5–6 (NIV): "Trust in the Lord with all your heart and lean not on your own understanding." When life did not make sense, she trusted God anyway. When situations looked impossible, she prayed. When answers were unclear, she waited with faith.

Magnolia taught prayer as a relationship, not a ritual. She lived Philippians 4:6–7, inviting people to bring every concern to God with honesty and trust. She believed prayer was the exchange of human weakness for divine strength. And she taught that God always hears, always sees, and always responds.

Even toward the end of her life, when her memory faded, and names slipped away, her relationship with God did not. She remembered the name of Jesus when she could not remember ours. She remembered Scripture when she could not recall time or place. She remembered prayer when her body grew tired. Her Spirit stood tall even when her body weakened. She remained a watchman on the wall until her final days.

She wanted everyone to know that salvation was not complicated. It was not unreachable. It was not something earned through performance. Salvation was a gift — a Father extending His arms, a Savior offering forgiveness, a Spirit offering comfort and companionship.

Magnolia didn't want us to have religion. She wanted us to have relationship.

She taught that religion can make you disciplined, but only relationship can make you whole.

Religion can make you show up to church, but relationship makes you show up to God.

Magnolia standing next to her garden on West Baltimore Street.

Religion can make you memorize Scripture, but relationship makes Scripture come alive inside you.

To Magnolia, faith was never about rituals. It was about connection. It was about intimacy with a Father who listens, a Savior who understands, and a Spirit who comforts. She believed healing begins in relationship — when we let God see us, touch us, guide us, and love us.

Some of the most important lessons she ever taught me came when I was a child — small moments that shaped my entire understanding of God.

I remember being seven or eight years old, unsure how to pray or how to read the Bible. I didn't know how to talk to God, and I felt intimidated by Scripture. But Magnolia made it simple. She always made God simple, close, and accessible. She told me to take my Bible, stand beside my bed, hold it in my hands, and ask God to direct me. "Tell Him you want to hear from Him," she said. "Ask Him where He wants you to be."

Then she told me to drop the Bible onto my bed and start reading wherever it opened. Whether it was a word, a verse, or a whole chapter — she said God would meet me there.

And He did—every single time.

That simple act taught me one of the greatest truths of faith: God responds to invitation. Not perfection. Not performance. Invitation. My heart didn't need to be eloquent

— it just needed to be open. She was teaching me to posture myself to listen, to expect God to show up, and to trust that He would guide me even as a child.

She discipled through relationship. She taught through simplicity. She opened the door for me to encounter God, not just learn about Him.

There were also times when I struggled to memorize Scripture the way other children did. While others recited verses effortlessly, I stumbled. The words wouldn't stay in my mind, and I often felt embarrassed. But Magnolia never let me feel less. She looked at me and said, "Baby, it's not about memorizing it. Yes, it's wonderful if you can. But more importantly — did you store the message in your heart?"

To her, memorization was optional. Revelation was essential.

She cared more about whether Scripture touched me than whether I could repeat it word-for-word. She taught that Scripture becomes alive not when it is memorized but when it is internalized — when the truth settles into your heart and begins shaping your choices, your thoughts, your identity. She said, "Scripture is not about remembering every Word. It's about letting the Word remember you."

This is who she was — someone who led people gently into a relationship with God, never pressure, never shame, never performance. She taught me that God does not require perfection — He requires openness.

And through that openness, healing begins.

Magnolia understood that people carry wounds — some visible, some buried deep — and that only God could heal the places untouched by human hands. She wanted everyone she met to know that God's love could reach them, restore them, and renew them. She wanted them to know that healing was not a distant promise; it was a present invitation.

This chapter is her altar call, though she never needed a pulpit to give one. Her life stands as the invitation:

Come to Jesus.

Come as you are.

Come with your pain, your exhaustion, your questions, your fears.

Come with your broken pieces.

Come with what you cannot fix on your own.

Come with what you hide from the world.

Come with your longing to be whole.

"Cast all your cares upon Him, for He cares for you." (1 Peter 5:7 NIV)

Magnolia believed salvation was not an escape, but an embrace. Not obligation — but belonging. Not ritual — but relationship.

She taught that Jesus is not only Savior and Lord, but friend, healer, counselor, and refuge. The one who carries what we cannot. The One who stays when others leave. The One who heals wounds too deep for words.

Her legacy now invites every reader into that same relationship:

Let God heal you.

Let God hold you.

Let God lead you.

Let God love you into wholeness.

For the most significant inheritance she left was not material wealth, but spiritual wealth — a faith that still calls, still comforts, still points toward Christ.

Her legacy is this:

God is real.

God is near.

God hears you.

God loves you.

And God wants a relationship with you.

Magnolia's story is complete, but what God wants to do in your story is just beginning.

Because every evangelist plants seeds, they never get to see them bloom.

And Magnolia's seeds are still growing — in us, through us, and now through the readers of this book.

EPILOGUE

Two Truths Can Stand Together

Written by a grandson who was shaped by her prayers and faith:

On December 19, I was given one of the most challenging assignments God has ever entrusted to me.

Our family, spanning generations, at her 90th birthday party.

It was an assignment my grandmother had asked me to fulfill decades earlier, long before I became a minister, long before I was ordained, long before I fully understood what she was asking of me. She had quietly, intentionally, and with great faith placed the responsibility in my hands. She asked that when the time came, I would officiate her service. And she asked that what is usually a eulogy would instead be a lesson. She asked, but in essence, she told me.

At the time, I did not understand the weight of that request. I certainly did not understand the grace behind it. But she did.

My grandmother understood something deeply about life, faith, and worship. She believed that celebrating her life should never center on her alone, but should always point upward, to God. She knew her life was not her own. It was an offering—a testimony. An act of worship lived out day by day.

And so, on that day, standing before family, friends, and generations shaped by her love, I understood. Her service was not about death. It was about devotion.

As we gathered, stories began to unfold, stories of joy, of laughter, of strength, of consistency. People spoke of her faith. They spoke of her gentleness. They spoke of her quiet power. Over and over again, the same words surfaced. You never saw her frown. You never heard her speak negatively about anyone. You never saw her lose her composure. She was classy. She was graceful. She was a lady in every sense of the Word.

My Father stood and spoke with gratitude to the congregation and directed them to thank God for the 92 years we had with her. He spoke of her as a servant of the Most High who had completed her assignment, had now taken her rest, and reaffirmed that this was a moment of celebration for his mother.

As I stood there in the pulpit, I remembered a question I had once asked her: What do you want your legacy to be?

Her answer was simple, but profound. She wanted her legacy to be one that loved God thoroughly, pointed people to her Father, and invited others into the peace, joy, and salvation that come from a relationship with Him. She did not want people to admire her. She wanted them to know Him.

As I sat and wrote this book, I realized it was never meant to be just a record of her life. It was meant to be her testimony, a testimony of light that shone brightly in this world, healing many along the way. Every step she took left behind footprints marked by obedience, humility, and love. Her life consistently reflected the character of the Most High.

That day, one truth became very clear: two truths can coexist.

Yes, we mourn.

Yes, we grieve.

We grieve because we lost someone vital. Someone irreplaceable. Someone who was a pillar of our family, a covering, a source of wisdom, prayer, and stability.

But we also celebrate.

We celebrate because a faithful servant has entered rest.

We celebrate because we know exactly where she is.

We celebrate because we know who she is with.

We celebrate because her faith carried her all the way home.

Both truths stand together.

We mourn the loss of our mother and our grandmother.

And we rejoice in the rest of a servant who finished well.

At her service, poems were shared that captured what many of us had always known but perhaps never named. They reminded us that her life was a garden, carefully tended over decades. A place where seeds were planted intentionally, watered faithfully, protected wisely, and allowed to grow strong.

We are that garden.

Each of us carries something she planted. Faith. Strength. Discipline. Compassion. Wisdom. Prayer. Love. We were nurtured by her care, shaped by her example, and guided by her quiet instruction. She knew when to shield us and when to step back so we could learn to stand on our own. She understood that growth requires both protection and trust.

And now, we are the harvest.

We are living evidence of what she poured out. Generations shaped by her love, and generations still growing from what she deposited. Her garden did not end with her life. It multiplied through it.

Her message never changed. She wanted people to seek God, to know His love, to experience the freedom and salvation that come from simply allowing Him into their lives. She taught that it was never about religion. It was always about relationship.

You do not have to be perfect to come before the Father.

You do not have to know everything to seek Him.

You can make mistakes, and He will still love you.

He is perfect, so you do not have to be.

It was an honor to stand and deliver the lesson she asked for, a lesson I did not fully understand until the very end. A lesson about inner strength that comes from friendship with Jesus. A lesson about peace that flows from relationship, not performance.

My prayer is that this book serves as a living testimony to my grandmother, to who she was, how she lived, and what she deposited into everyone who crossed her path.

She was the woman who sat on her stoop nearly every morning at six o'clock, a cup of coffee in hand, surrounded by Bibles, prepared to speak to anyone who would stop about how good her Father is.

And even now, her life still speaks.

It still points upward.

It still invites hearts.

It still calls people into a relationship.

Her assignment is complete.

Her testimony remains.

MAGNOLIA'S PERSONAL
INVITATION TO YOU

Many people struggle to come to God, not because they do not believe, but because they are carrying wounds they do not know how to release. Some are carrying unforgiveness toward others. Some are carrying unforgiveness toward themselves. Some feel rejected, forgotten, or tossed aside. Some feel broken beyond repair. Some feel like they were never enough to be chosen, protected, or loved.

Magnolia understood this kind of pain. She believed that healing does not begin with pretending hurt never happened. Healing begins when we are honest about what wounded us and brave enough to place it in God's hands.

Forgiveness is not saying what happened was acceptable. Forgiveness is releasing yourself from carrying what was never meant to live inside you. Forgiveness is trusting God with justice so your heart can finally rest.

There are people who hurt you and never apologized.

There are people who left when you needed them most.

There are words spoken over you that still echo in your mind.

There are moments you replay, wishing you had been stronger, wiser, different.

And there are ways you have turned that pain inward, convincing yourself that you were the problem, that you were unlovable, that you were not enough.

But God never said you were disposable.

He never said you were forgotten.

He never said you were too broken to heal.

Scripture tells us, "He heals the brokenhearted and binds up their wounds" (Psalm 147:3). That includes wounds caused by others and wounds caused by our own self-condemnation.

Magnolia believed forgiveness was an act of freedom. She believed releasing bitterness made room for peace. She believed loving yourself as God loves you was not pride, but obedience. You cannot walk in wholeness while agreeing with lies spoken over you.

Self-love, in its truest form, is not selfishness. It is agreeing with God about your worth. It is seeing yourself through the lens of grace instead of shame. It is allowing God to love you into healing places you have kept hidden.

If you are feeling alone, God is near.

If you feel rejected, know that God has chosen you and will always choose you.

If you feel broken, God restores.

If you feel forgotten, God remembers.

And if you are carrying guilt, shame, or regret, forgiveness is available to you right now.

As Scripture reminds us, "Cast all your cares upon Him, for He cares for you" (1 Peter 5:7).

You were never meant to carry this alone.

God invites us just as we are.

If you desire to begin or renew a relationship with Him, you can do so right now, exactly where you are. There is no special posture required. No perfect words needed. Only an open heart.

If you feel led, you may pray this prayer.

A PRAYER OF SURRENDER, HEALING, AND RENEWAL

Father God,

I come to You just as I am.

I bring every part of me that is tired, wounded, confused, or unsure.

I acknowledge that I need You, not only for salvation, but for healing and restoration.

I believe that You love me completely.

I believe that Jesus Christ is Your Son,

That He lived, died, and rose again

So that I could have life, peace, freedom, and wholeness.

I confess that there are wounds I have carried for a long time.

Pain caused by others.

Pain caused by words spoken over me.

Pain caused by rejection, abandonment, abuse, neglect, or loss.

Today, I choose to release what I have been holding.
I forgive those who hurt me, even when they never apologized.
I release resentment, bitterness, and anger into Your hands.
I trust You with justice so my heart can finally rest.

And Father, I also ask You to help me forgive myself.
For the mistakes I regret.
For the shame I have carried.
For believing I was not enough.
For agreeing with lies that You never spoke.

I renounce every lie that says I am disposable, forgotten,
broken beyond repair, or unworthy of love.
I receive Your truth instead.
That I am chosen.
That I am seen.
That I am loved.

Jesus, I invite You into my life.
Not only as Savior,
But as a friend.
Walk with me.
Heal me.
Teach me how to trust You with my whole heart.

I surrender my burdens, my fears, my past, and my future to
You.
I receive Your forgiveness, Your grace, Your peace, and Your
presence.
Restore what has been worn down.
Heal what has been broken.
Renew what has grown dim.

Help me to love myself the way You love me.
Not with pride, but with truth.
Not with shame, but with grace.
Help me to live rooted in who You say I am.

From this moment forward,
I choose relationship over religion,
faith over fear,
And trust over control.

Thank You for receiving me.
Thank You for healing me.
Thank You for walking with me.
Thank You for never letting me go.

Amen.

If you have prayed this prayer, the journey does not end here. In many ways, it has only begun. Faith is not a moment. It is a daily choice to walk with God, one step at a time. Magnolia often reminded us that God honors willingness more than perfection. You do not need to know everything. You only need to keep showing up with an open heart.

The next step is simple: make space for God in your everyday life. Talk to Him honestly. Read His Word, even if you do not understand everything at first. Let Scripture speak to you where you are. As Magnolia taught, it is not about memorizing verses as much as it is about storing truth in your heart. Ask God to guide you, and trust that He will meet you in what you read and when you pray.

You will also need community. Faith was never meant to be lived alone. Finding a church home and people you can fellowship with helps strengthen your walk and supports your growth in a relationship with God. Surround yourself with others who pray with you, walk alongside you, and encourage you in truth and love. At the same time, extend grace to yourself. Healing is a process. Growth takes time. God is patient, and His love does not diminish when you struggle.

Finally, let your life become a reflection of what you are receiving. Share love where there is hurt. Offer kindness where there is need. Pray when you feel led, even if the words feel small. Plant seeds wherever you go and trust God to bring the growth. As Magnolia lived and taught, a life rooted in faith will always bear fruit in its season.